A Note to Paren

DK READERS is a compelling program for beginning readers, designed in conjunction with leading literacy experts, including Dr. Linda Gambrell, Professor of Education at Clemson University. Dr. Gambrell has served as President of the National Reading Conference and the College Reading Association, and has recently been elected to serve as President of the International Reading Association.

Beautiful illustrations and superb full-color photographs combine with engaging, easy-to-read stories to offer a fresh approach to each subject in the series. Each DK READER is guaranteed to capture a child's interest while developing his or her reading skills, general knowledge, and love of reading.

The five levels of DK READERS are aimed at different reading abilities, enabling you to choose the books that are exactly right for your child:

Pre-level 1: Learning to read
Level 1: Beginning to read
Level 2: Beginning to read alone
Level 3: Reading alone
Level 4: Proficient readers

The "normal" age at which a child begins to read can be anywhere from three to eight years old. Adult participation through the lower levels is very helpful for providing encouragement, discussing storylines, and sounding out unfamiliar words.

No matter which level you select, you can be sure that you are helping your child learn to read, then read to learn!

LONDON, NEW YORK, MUNICH,
MELBOURNE, AND DELHI

For Dorling Kindersley
Senior Editor Laura Gilbert
Managing Art Editor Ron Stobbart
Publishing Manager Catherine Saunders
Art Director Lisa Lanzarini
Associate Publisher Simon Beecroft
Category Publisher Alex Allan
Production Editor Sean Daly
Production Controller Rita Sinha
Reading Consultant Dr. Linda Gambrell

For Lucasfilm
Executive Editor J. W. Rinzler
Art Director Troy Alders
Keeper of the Holocron Leland Chee
Director of Publishing Carol Roeder

Designed and edited by Tall Tree Ltd
Designer Sandra Perry
Editor Jon Richards

First published in the United States in 2011
by DK Publishing
375 Hudson Street, New York, New York 10014

11 12 13 14 15 10 9 8 7 6 5 4 3 2 1

DK books are available at special discounts when purchased in bulk
for sales promotions, premiums, fund-raising, or educational use.
For details, contact:
DK Publishing Special Markets
375 Hudson Street
New York, New York 10014
SpecialSales@dk.com

A catalog record for this book is available
from the Library of Congress.

ISBN: 978-0-7566-8280-4 (Hardback)
ISBN: 978-0-7566-8281-1 (Paperback)

Reproduced by Media Development and Printing Ltd., UK
Printed and bound in China by L.Rex Printing Company Ltd.

Discover more at:
www.dk.com
www.starwars.com

Contents

DK READERS

STAR WARS®

THE CLONE WARS™

BOBA FETT:
JEDI HUNTER

Clare Hibbert

Who is that angry boy?

It is Boba Fett.

Boba wants to hunt down a Jedi
Master called Mace Windu.

During a battle, Windu struck
down Boba's father, who was
called Jango Fett.
Now Boba wants revenge.
Can a boy fight a Jedi?
Boba is no ordinary boy.

Jedi Master
Mace Windu is a
powerful Jedi Master.
He can use the Force
to give himself
special powers.

Boba is a bounty hunter.
Bounty hunters are paid to
track down people.
Boba works with Aurra Sing.

Teamwork
Aurra and Boba team up with other
bounty hunters. Castas is big and
strong. He uses a blaster pistol.

Aurra is a bounty hunter, too.

She is one of the boldest hunters.

She will help Boba find

Mace Windu.

Aurra Sing

These are clone troopers.

Clones are exact copies of other living beings.

The troopers are clones of Jango.

Jango asked to keep one clone to bring up as his own son.

This son is Boba Fett.

Clone planet

The clones are trained at a special base
on the planet of Kamino.
Kamino is covered with seas and oceans.

A group called the Separatists
wants to leave the Republic.
Jango helps the Separatists and
their droid soldiers.
The Separatists fight many battles
against the clone troopers.

Mace Windu uses his lightsaber to strike down Jango, Boba's father, during one of these battles.

Jango's helmet

After Jango's death, Boba picks up his father's helmet. He swears to take revenge against Mace Windu!

Aurra has an idea.

She knows how Boba can get close
to Windu. He must pretend to be
a clone cadet.

It is risky pretending to be
something you are not,
but Boba is very determined.
No one can stand in his way.

Boba joins Sergeant Crasher's cadet unit. Crasher teaches the cadets how to be troopers. He makes sure that the best cadets have extra training.

Clone commanders

The best clone troopers become commanders, like Commander Wolffe. He is a brilliant leader. His troops will do anything for him.

Boba needs to wear a special cadet uniform to blend in. When cadets are training on Kamino, they wear cadet armor.

Sometimes, clone cadets wear a gray shirt with a leather belt and boots.

Insignia

Clone uniforms have special badges called insignia. Commander Wolffe's men wear an insignia of a wolf's head.

Some cadets try to bully Boba.
Jax tells them to leave Boba alone.
He is a good leader. He tries to
make friends with Boba.

Jax

Jax doesn't know that Boba is
not what he seems.
He doesn't know that Boba is on
a mission to hunt down a Jedi.

Before Jango died, he taught Boba
everything he knew.
Boba is a very good shot.
He blasts away with the cannon
on the starship *Endurance*.

The Jedi Generals Obi-Wan
Kenobi and Mace Windu are
also on the *Endurance*. Boba is
pleased. His hunt is nearly over!
He may soon have his revenge.

Cannon

After Jango died, Boba inherited his spaceship. It is called *Slave I*. Boba has been flying it for years. He is now an ace pilot. But who is flying it while Boba is hunting Mace Windu on board the *Endurance*?

Boba's ship

Slave I used
to be a ship for
transporting prisoners.
Jango also used it to
transport slaves across
the galaxy. It is full of
the weapons a bounty
hunter needs.

Boba is an expert with gadgets. He has a secret comlink to talk to the other bounty hunters. He uses powerful binoculars to track down Mace Windu.

Trapping a Jedi
Boba uses his father's helmet as a trap. Jedi Knight Anakin doesn't know there is a bomb inside. However, Windu manages to save Anakin.

Boba has no luck on board the *Endurance.* He must find another way to catch the Jedi.

Aurra commands Boba to destroy the *Endurance*. The cadets climb inside an escape pod to get out of the *Endurance*. Another ship comes to the rescue. It is *Slave I.* It is being flown by bounty hunters!

No mercy

You have to be tough to be a bounty hunter. Aurra gives Boba a difficult choice: abandon the cadets in space or stay with them in the escape pod and die.

Boba will try anything to get his revenge. He will even take hostages. He captures some of the crew from the *Endurance*.

Mace Windu and Anakin try to rescue the hostages, but they walk into a trap. A bomb explodes. The Jedi barely escape.

Now it is Boba's turn to be hunted.
Jedi Master Plo Koon is looking for
the young bounty hunter.
Boba puts up a good fight,
but Plo Koon is too powerful.

Plo Koon takes Boba to Coruscant.
Boba is face to face with Mace
Windu once again, but this time
Boba is a prisoner.
He failed this time, but this bold
bounty hunter will be back.
Watch your step, Jedi!

Glossary

cadet
A person who is training to be a soldier.

clone trooper
A soldier built to serve the Republic.

comlink
A mobile device that transmits voice signals.

escape pod
A small craft used to escape from a larger craft that is in trouble.

Force
A power that flows through the galaxy.

hostage
Someone who is kept prisoner as a way to bargain with the enemy.

Jedi
A warrior who fights for good.

lightsaber
A swordlike weapon with a blade of pure energy.